How I Learned To Sing

A complete guide to creating stronger
performances with dynamic vocal technique

Jonathan E. Smith

Copyright Page

Copyright © 2020 by Jonathan E. Smith
How I Learned To Sing

All rights reserved. No part of this publication may be reproduced, distributed or transmitted in any form or by any means, including photocopying, recording, or other electronic or mechanical methods, without the prior written permission of the publisher, except in the case of brief quotations embodied in critical reviews and certain other noncommercial uses permitted by copyright law.

Although the author and publisher have made every effort to ensure that the information in this book was correct at press time, the author and publisher do not assume and hereby disclaim any liability to any party for any loss, damage, or disruption caused by errors or omissions, whether such errors or omissions result from negligence, accident, or any other cause.

Adherence to all applicable laws and regulations, including international, federal, state and local governing professional licensing, business practices, advertising, and all other aspects of doing business in the US, Canada or any other jurisdiction is the sole responsibility of the reader and consumer.

Neither the author nor the publisher assumes any responsibility or liability whatsoever on behalf of the consumer or reader of this material. Any per-ceived slight of any individual or organization is purely unintentional.

The resources in this book are provided for informational purposes only and should not be used to replace the specialized training and professional judgment of a health care or mental health care professional.

Neither the author nor the publisher can be held responsible for the use of the information provided within this book. Please always consult a trained professional before making any decision regarding treatment of yourself or others.

ISBN: 978-1-7354395-0-1

Dedication

This book is dedicated to everyone who has a dream, myself included. I used to believe that talent was something you were only born with. I can't begin to tell you how wrong I was. Throughout my life, time and time again, life has proven to me that by combining your dreams with focus, discipline, strategic effort, and love for yourself and others, you have access to the supernatural wonders of the world. It's all just waiting for you to truly believe in yourself and take that first step. For many of you, these pages will be your first steps and I'm immensely grateful for the opportunity to walk with you.

I Have A Gift For You!

If you're anything like me, you probably love free stuff!

As a way to say thanks for purchasing this book, I want to give you the free How I Learned To Sing vocal checklist.

HOW I LEARNED TO SING VOCAL CHECKLIST

1.
2.
3.
4.
5.
6.
7.

I use this as a guide for my warm ups and a pre-performance check-in with my mind and body. I guarantee if you implement this list in your daily singing routine, you will notice improvement very quickly!

You can download the list by visiting
http://officialjonathanesmith.com/singerschecklist

Thank you so much for your support!

I believe I have, inside of me, everything that I need to live a bountiful life. With all the love alive in me, I will stand as tall as the tallest tree.

— "I'm Here" from *The Color Purple Musical*

TABLE OF CONTENTS

	Introduction	1
I	Technique	4
II	Release of Tension	8
III	Posture	13
IV	Breathing	15
V	Voices & Registers	20
VI	Intonation	23
VII	Cord Closure	26
VIII	Resonance	32
IX	Larynx	37
X	Mix/Middle Voice	41
XI	Diction	44
XII	Singing and the Mind	46
XIII	Random Thoughts	51

INTRODUCTION

Whew…
Thanks for buying this book!

    I'm sitting in my bed, starting this, on January 16th, 2020. I'm telling you that because I think it'll be really cool to see where I am when this actually comes out. At this moment, I have no idea how to write or publish a book, but I do know how to sing, and at 25 years old, I'd like to think that I have a pretty consistent and reliable singing voice. Is my voice perfect? Absolutely not. Are there flaws? Definitely. Believe it or not, there are flaws and inconsistencies in everyone's voice. However, I will say that I've developed a speaking and singing voice that I'm proud of. Pleasing, strong, colorful, controlled, beautiful, and even sexy are just a few words that people have used to describe my voice, and, by no means, am I saying this to toot my own horn. This is all to say that I have researched, practiced, strategized, and created a voice that I'm confident will make sounds that sit well in the human ear. You know what else? You can too, and I'm gonna teach you how!
    Before I begin, let me clarify that this book isn't designed to be a foolproof guide. I won't market this as an end-all-be-all guide to amazingness. This book is solely me, Jay Smith, detailing my journey and what has worked for me as a vocal performer. I'll also detail my findings as a voice teacher, based on the improvements I notice in my current pool of students. I definitely encourage singers to work with a coach and research voice anatomy and technique in their own time, which you're scratching the surface of just by reading this book. Go you!
    If you're reading this, I'm willing to bet you fall into a few different categories: you may be a proficient singer who wants

to continue your education on the craft. You may be self-taught and want to have some concrete knowledge on different technical aspects. You may have absolutely no experience singing at all and want to learn a brand-new skill. Regardless of what category you fall into, I'm invested in giving you an array of awarenesses that have worked for me in my singing journey and for many students whom I teach regularly.

I wasn't always a good singer and I definitely had to learn to sing efficiently. My dream of having a singing voice that people would enjoy listening to is what made me so disciplined in the journey to learn more and improve my instrument. For me, singing with unstable and inconsistent technique wasn't an option, so I made it a point to *ambitiously* learn the anatomy of the voice and how to manipulate it. Therefore, remember: *ambition makes up where talent lacks*. If you have the unrelenting desire to sing well, you have to imagine the voice you want, learn about the qualities of it, and work at it. One day, you'll hear yourself and realize that you're pleased with how it feels to sing. (*Ask me how I know!*) I find that this also applies to anything and everything in life. If you want success in any field, you must analyze, strategize, believe the success to be possible, and relentlessly chase your goal until you have achieved it. Learning to sing taught me that with dedication, focus, and strategic effort, I'm capable of learning anything; I truly hope you believe the same about yourself.

In this book, I'll tell you my understanding of vocal technique, some of my previous vocal faults and how I overcame them, plus my personal dos and don'ts for anyone who wants to be able to use their instrument consistently and for long stretches of time. By the time you reach the last chapter, I'll just include random tips and talking points. (*I loooove when books do that!*)

Your journey in singing won't be exactly like mine, so we'll have some crossovers and some crossroads, but the beauty lies in the fact that you have the ultimate say for how you want to sound. The concepts in this book are what worked for me and I hope that through explanation, they also work for you.

I. TECHNIQUE

Many voice books brand themselves as the "only way," and I think that's dangerous because people are extremely different in various ways. This became evident to me when I began teaching multiple students the same concepts. I graduated with a Bachelor's in Voice Performance and immediately began working for a small music studio in Cornelius, NC. Having never taught before, I felt it necessary to learn all I could about singing out of fear of teaching someone technique that would damage their instrument. I would research different exercises, practice them myself, and try to apply them to all ten of my students in a day, six days a week.

What I learned from this was that many of the exercises that benefit 14-year-old Joseph, whose voice is going through puberty, won't equally benefit 54-year-old Lisa, who sings karaoke and just wants to improve her voice to sing at her friend's wedding. (*Yes, these are real people and situations I was faced with.*) Nevertheless, the foundations of stable singing transcend from person to person, and this is where technique comes into play.

What Is Technique?

This may seem remedial, but simply put, technique is the *way* you sing. I used to get so hung up on having "perfect" technique that I began to overthink singing to the point that it hindered my progress. I teach my students that if you're producing the sounds you want without tension or pain and you could confidently recreate those sounds 6 to 7 times a week, you have good, solid technique.

Only in rare circumstances should you be thinking about your technique during a performance. If you find yourself thinking about technique on stage, this is a sign that you haven't drilled the technique enough during your practice.

Practicing technique is just that: practice. This spans across all media and applications. A dancer isn't practicing their stretches on opening night. A basketball player isn't testing his free throws in the middle of a game. Likewise, singers don't practice their breathing and scales on the opening night of their showcase. We practice diligently off stage so that a smooth performance becomes second nature. The ultimate goal is to have your technique so well practiced that you no longer have to be aware of it. Your technique should be a part of your muscle memory.

Not too long ago, I came down with a cold the morning of an important gig and I couldn't cancel or find a replacement in time. Obviously, this was a less-than-ideal situation, especially seeing as how I had written and arranged many of the songs to show off the highs of my voice, which were virtually gone that morning. Even though I was sick, the *way* I went about producing my voice didn't change for that performance, but I definitely had to be a bit more aware of it due to my temporary impediment.

At times, you will have strategically practiced and warmed up your voice and an unforeseen factor will alter the production quality of your tone. Some of these factors include but aren't limited to: humidity levels, the temperature, how loud or quiet it is in the venue, pollen levels and air quality in the city, and secondhand smoke. Situations like these can impact your performance, making you feel like you didn't reach your optimal potential, and that's okay. Once you're aware of something that may be a hindrance, don't panic. Panic causes shallow breathing and tension in the throat and neck. Just stay calm and slightly adjust accordingly. There's no such thing as a perfect performance.

So, how did I develop healthy and consistent technique? Through trial, error, and listening to my body. If singing hurts, you're absolutely doing something wrong and should immediately stop. If you leave the stage feeling like you have a loss in range, you need to review your performance and make some adjustments in your practice because, though your voice is magnificently resilient, over time, exercising bad habits will catch up to you.

Components of Technique

We'll dive into the specifics of the following terms later in this book, but the main components of vocal technique and control are as follows:

- **Release of Tension**: Removing all tightness in the body.
- **Posture**: How you align your body to sing.
- **Breathing**: Engaging your diaphragm without activating your chest and neck
- **Different Voices or Registers**: Various ways to identify high and low
- **Intonation**: How well you hear pitches and recreate them with your voice
- **Cord Closure**: How much air you allow to pass through your vocal folds
- **Resonance**: Where you feel your voice vibrating in your head and face
- **Larynx**: How high or low your "voice box" sits in your throat
- **Diction**: How clearly you pronounce your lyrics
- **The Mind**: How you mentally and spiritually interact with the music

Except for breathing, posture, and intonation, I believe there are no "golden rules" when it comes to these terms. As I stated before, the two questions you must ask yourself when building technique are "am I making the sounds I want without strain or tension?" and "can I recreate these sounds on command?" These two questions leave you in the driver's seat. Instead of stressing over if you're singing correctly, you rejoice in the ability to sing the way you want to.

When I first began singing, I strictly sang from emotion. I had absolutely no concept of technique at all. I just knew that I enjoyed how the act of singing made me feel. However, I also realized that people didn't typically respond well to the sound of my voice. When I would ask for feedback, people would often say things like "I like your lyrics" or "I see what you were going for," but rarely would people actually say, "That was beautiful" or "I love the sound of your voice." At this point, I can admit that even I didn't like the sound of my own voice.

This really bothered me because I listened to popular singers like Whitney Houston and Frank Sinatra belt these immensely powerful notes with ease and emotion and I wanted to be able to do the same. Since I grew up in church, I knew many singers who never took lessons and I was in awe of how these people sang so well, so "naturally." Now, after training my voice for almost a decade, I have realized that the number of singers who are "naturals" is objectively small.

When you encounter someone who's a "naturally good singer," you're actually witnessing a naturally intuitive learner, someone who has unknowingly practiced and reinforced consistent technique early in their singing journey. Many times, this person has grown up hearing people make sounds that were appealing to their ears. This could be a family or community member, a church choir, or even a famous singer on the radio. Regardless, they have found a way to mimic those attractive sounds in their own special and unique way.

They were not born with a magical voice. They were born with a set of vocal cords, a diaphragm, and stories to tell, just like who? YOU! If you get familiar with the concepts in this book and learn how to manipulate them in your own body, you may not sound like Whitney Houston or Frank Sinatra, but you can certainly improve your performances and sing with strength, flexibility, and confident energy like they did.

Now… onto the specifics!

II. RELEASE OF TENSION

Our goal when warming up our voices should be to release tension. Tension is the root of all evil in singing, so you must disengage tense muscles before you even begin producing tone. When I find myself struggling to vocalize a certain pitch, I notice that a source of tension is hindering my airflow. Oddly enough, tension has a covert way of disguising itself as support at times. When singing, the places we tend to carry tension the most are the tongue, jaw, neck, and torso/abdominal muscles.

Releasing the Tongue

The tongue is an interesting muscle because it gets tense in the most imperceptible ways. When I just can't seem to access higher notes in my range, I often find that my tongue is getting caught in the back of my throat. An easy way to fix this when practicing or warming up is to simply stick your tongue out as far as it will go. The tongue root can't stiffen up if you're actively releasing it forward. Vocalizing in this position is also very helpful because it trains your body to produce tone with lots of space near the tongue root, pharynx, and soft palate.

Another helpful tip is to stretch your tongue out of your mouth in as many different directions as possible prior to and during your warm ups. I compare this to how dancers stretch their entire bodies before beginning a workout or doing choreography. They stretch in many different ways, making sure not to leave any muscle group overlooked. In a way, our tongue is the dancer of our mouths. Since it's the main articulator that forms all our words, we have to be diligent about loosening up this extremely hard-working muscle.

My current coach, David Clark, once told me that you should feel like you have a "mouthful of tongue." I find that this not only keeps the tongue present but releases the jaw as well. With this in mind, I try to keep the tip of my tongue touching the back of my bottom lip, especially when warming up. Anything you can do to prevent the tongue root from stiffening and closing off your airflow in the back of your mouth should aid you in your vocal production.

The Jaw
Whew...

The more you learn about the voice and interact with other singers, the more you'll find that every singer on Earth has their own set of strengths and challenges to their voice. For me, jaw tension is one of the main culprits that I'm constantly addressing. For years, I wanted my singing to convey a sense of yearning. Many of my songs portray a tone of needing the subject to believe me, demanding to be desired or the like, but I was achieving this tone in an uncomfortable way. So many of my songs relied on the sound being achieved with a tense jaw, and I never realized that there were more sustainable ways to achieve that same goal. A general rule to remember is that whatever sound you're trying to make, there's a healthy, sustainable way to achieve it. Don't tax your voice just because you want to sound a certain way and you only know one way to do it. If singing ever becomes uncomfortable, learn how to make it comfortable.

Releasing the Jaw

Jaw tension typically lies in the jaw hinge located directly in front of the earlobe. A good way to release tension here's by placing a thumb on your chin and pushing your jaw down until your mouth opens tall and you feel your jaw hinge stretch. Do not allow the tongue to retract backward in the process. I never realize how much tension I've been holding in this area until I remove my hand and feel how loose my jaw is afterwards. I have started doing this stretch as part of my morning routine as well, just to keep my jaw generally loose throughout the day.

Massaging my jaw hinge for 60 seconds on each side generally helps too. Our bodies always feel like jello after a massage, so it would only make sense that our jaw would feel relaxed and loose after a minute of this attention. A young student of mine reported that they alternate between stretching and massaging and this gave them really good results.

Regardless of how much our jaw actually moves in song, it should have the freedom to move up and down when pronouncing words, like that of a ventriloquist's dummy. When we create more space for higher and lower pitches, we often forget that our jaw is an integral part in allowing the proper amount of airflow to be released. It is almost impossible to expel your air into higher tones, specifically belts/mix, without opening your mouth and creating adequate space.

Releasing the Neck

The neck is another mysterious cause of tension that often goes unnoticed. For me, the best way to release neck tension is by slowly rolling the neck around clockwise for 30 to 60 seconds or until relaxed. Next, repeat the same motion counterclockwise. Another similar method is a slow, exaggerated "no" motion. Turn your head to the left so that your chin touches your shoulder, then repeat on the other side.

Neck tension can also be an indicator of poor breath support. This is why learning to properly breathe is so important! If you feel your outer neck muscles engaging when you inhale, this is a sign that the diaphragm isn't fully taking in air. This will make the diaphragm feel the need to "call on" the neck muscles to help do its job, but, in reality, the neck muscles are doing more harm than good. Once you learn to confidently take in air deeply, you should notice that your neck is employed less and less.

If the neck muscles engage during vocalizing, you may not be confidently releasing all your air into the mask, which I'll be talking about in the chapters on breathing and the mask. When air is fully released, it feels similar to a sigh. When we sigh after a long day, our necks don't tense around our larynx.

Refer to the section on breathing for further info. If you notice that you have a tendency to tense your neck while you sing, try vocalizing on a strong "hmm," while doing the neck roll and "exaggerated no" exercises from earlier and make a mental note of how it feels to use your voice as the neck disengages and ultimately, relaxes.

Releasing the Torso/Abdominals

The general region of our torso and abdominals play a key role in our singing because it's where our lungs and diaphragm are located. Therefore, tension in this area affects our entire breathing mechanism and can constrict our singing quite a bit. When I have tension in this area, it hinders my breathing by not allowing the breath cycle to efficiently take place. A way that I combat this is to remind myself that the abdominals are released and relaxed during my inhale. My midsection should be free to expand on all sides during the intake of breath. If my stomach is tight, I notice that my diaphragm doesn't drop into place and allow an adequate amount of air into my lungs. When I exhale, my abs and diaphragm slowly contract inward on their own, but only if I sing with balanced cord closure. If I allow an excess amount of air to pass through the vocal cords, I notice my abs and diaphragm come in faster because more breath is leaving my lungs.

Personally, the Farinelli exercise works well for releasing tension and pressure from my torso. It focuses solely on relaxing your body while managing the breath cycle. You can find information on this exercise in the chapter about breathing.

III. POSTURE

An old acquaintance once said, "You'll never be completely sure of where you're going if you're never in the right alignment." Granted, this person was detailing alignment in sort of a spiritual, life-path way, but this also applies to the body's posture for singing. If your body isn't aligned properly, your breath cannot travel where it needs to go as easily. Aligned posture supports relaxation of the body, which allows for free and comfortable movement, internally and externally.

I like to take a sort of spiritual approach when thinking of my posture. I believe that my posture should keep me grounded and stable to the earth. I almost imagine myself being firmly planted like a tree. When my feet are shoulder-width apart, my weight is equally balanced; this keeps me stable in my stance. My Queens University voice teacher, Connie Rhyne, once gently pushed me on both sides to see if I would clumsily tip over. Fortunately, I didn't.

If we continue taking this same approach in terms of posture, we can learn a lot about alignment as well. For instance, if our tree bends too much in one spot, it will snap and tumble over. This would disconnect the tree from its roots, its only source of life energy. In relation to my body, if there are any places that are interrupting my alignment, this disrupts the relationship between me and my source of life energy: the breath. Once I became aware of singing with a tall, elongated spine, I found it easier to control my breath because this alignment allows room for efficient breath cycles.

The order in which Connie originally taught me alignment goes as such. My feet stand shoulder-width apart. My knees aren't bent backwards, as this notoriously cuts off the blood supply to the rest of the body. In fact, I keep my knees slightly bent (*in case I feel like bouncing to the music*). Next, I bend over and touch my toes, then very slowly roll back up, feeling each disc of my spine stack one on the other until I reach the nape of my neck. Lastly, I sit my head atop the nape of my neck, making sure to have my chin slightly down. Kristin Linklater, author of *Freeing the Natural Voice*, provides the image of the head floating over the rest of your body like a balloon. This image helped me keep the back of my neck elongated and my chin lowered as well.

Sometimes, when our relationship to alignment isn't stable or when we begin to sing passages that touch us emotionally, our jaws begin to jut forward, causing our external neck muscles to activate. Keeping your head in this general "floating" place really helps to clean up tension in the throat and neck. However, for me, it's imperative to remember the emphasis of *floating* like a balloon. If I don't actively view my skull as a floating balloon, my neck can involuntarily get tense.

One helpful thing that my coach, David, tells me is to imagine that my spine and torso are continuously elongating as the phrase I'm singing goes on. Working this thought process into warm ups keeps my spine tall, and I'm able to confidently stand straight. By meditating on this image in my practice and working it into my muscle memory, the action of an elongated neck and strong posture will become an unconscious habit.

IV. BREATHING

Why do we practice breathing?

In my teachings, singing is nothing more than the release of breath combined with some sort of vocal cord connection. Great singing is being able to control the breath and express the emotions and stories you want with it. I've taken lessons from a handful of teachers and, except for one, they all taught breathing technique. Unfortunately, not all my teachers explained the purpose of breathing exercises, leaving me too much room for error when it came to breathing. In my own teachings, I've found that, oftentimes, if a student knows the reason for an exercise, they'll make a unique connection to the end goal and come up with a subjective way of getting there. This is the beauty of teaching many students because one student will often come up with something that will help you communicate differently to others. But I digress. Back to breathing!

The purpose of breathing exercises is to focus all your energy below the lower ribcage. Contrary to common belief, this is where the act of singing takes place. Many people believe that breathing into the chest or activating your throat muscles helps you sing better, but, put plainly, this is just false. You can make minor adjustments in these places, such as lowering the larynx, but singing consistently and for long stretches of time is only possible if you learn to govern and control your voice from beneath the low ribs.

Breathing exercises are designed to teach your diaphragm how to descend, making adequate room for your lungs to take in air quickly and quietly. After your lungs have taken in the air, you have an almost seamless moment of suspension, then finally you exhale, causing your diaphragm to contract inward, quickly sending the air upward, through the vocal cords and out of the vocal tract. This is the diaphragmatic engagement that allows you to sing long passages without feeling like you have to gasp for new air.

Although I'm aware of what people mean, there's no such thing as "singing from the diaphragm." Your vocal cords aren't located on your diaphragm and the act of tone production doesn't take place there. When people use this phrase, they really mean "engage your diaphragm, while breathing." When you inhale, your lower torso should expand on all sides. This includes the abdominals, obliques, and the lower back. Students tend to respond well when I tell them to imagine holding a balloon upside down and seeing it inflate with air. When you inhale, your lower rib cage and lower back should also expand outward and your general pelvic area should expand downward. Your upper ribs and chest SHOULD NOT expand at all.

Breathing

Breathing IN — lungs, trachea, diaphragm — Inspiration

Breathing OUT — lungs, trachea, diaphragm — Exhalation

Below are a few exercises that have taught me to control my breath. At least one should be practiced daily.

The Farinelli Exercise

My absolute favorite exercise that still surprises me when I find myself mindlessly reaping its benefits is the Farinelli exercise. My college voice teacher, Connie, also referred to this as the "sixteen seconds of relaxation." Personally, since I started using it, I haven't had to practice diaphragm training exercises as much. The Farinelli exercise teaches your diaphragm the breath cycle for singing in three equal phases. This is the process of taking in air for four seconds, suspending the breath with the throat open for four, exhaling for four seconds, then a final four second suspension before inhaling again.

There are two main things to remember when doing this exercise:

1. Don't take in too much air. It's definitely possible to over-inhale, which is why you're limited to a four-second inhale. When you over-inhale, you create too much of something called "subglottal pressure." This is pressure beneath your "glottis," which is the space where your vocal cords lie. In simpler terms, too much backed up air pressure beneath your throat will result in an extremely tight/squeezed sound when you start to sing. Remember to comfortably and quietly inhale into the lower belly/back for four seconds.

2. You must keep your throat open. Notice I didn't say "holding" the breath. I specifically said "suspending." When breath is suspended, the throat and glottis remain open, which is arguably the most important factor of this exercise. When you inhale through your mouth, your throat automatically opens for you. Your job is to keep this open throat while there's no air passing in or out. I had a student tell me once, "It feels like if someone threw popcorn in my mouth, it would fly all the way down to my stomach." When the glottis remains open, the diaphragm is forced to

continue working to suspend the inhale. If you close off your throat, you let the diaphragm off the hook. Remember: the purpose of breathing exercises is to train the diaphragm! After these two steps, you exhale as normal and repeat the cycle until you can do this type of breathing on command with no hesitation.

Panting

One simple activity that I had no idea worked so well, so quickly is rapidly inhaling and exhaling with your tongue out. It helps to imagine an exhausted dog that has just finished going for a walk. This exercise is designed to quickly focus your energy into your lower abdomen and help create sort of a "reference point" for where your breath, and eventually your singing, should come from. This breathing exercise is no different than others in that it only benefits you if your abdominals, obliques, and back muscles expand while you inhale and contract while you exhale.

Just like the Farinelli exercise, I find that panting is an amazing gateway into singing because once I feel my breath is solely entering and releasing from my lower abdomen, I simply replace the exhale with any note that's comfortable for me. This exercise really revitalized my singing voice because it taught me to allow my vocal production to come from a much deeper place than I was originally used to.

The Two Rs

Recently, I've developed a thought pattern that has worked well for many of my students. I refer to this system as *The Two Rs–replenish and release.* This is where you mentally give your breath cycle two functions. The function of your inhale is to replenish your body with air and energy (life) for the upcoming phrase. You must enjoy each deep inhale and teach your body and mind to feel peaceful every time you take one. They're subtle reminders that you're allowed to continue expressing what you feel. What a joy!

Your exhale is there to release the breath energy in the form of expression. I find that people sing the most efficiently when they exhale quickly, yet comfortably. I often have my students let out a string of loud "shhh" sounds, as if they're in the movies and someone is talking on their phone. I teach my students to release their breath this way because it keeps their lungs, diaphragm, and brain extremely active. I notice an immediate improvement once they begin to sing. Their voices are clearer, more energetic, and more engaged with the lyrics. The main thing to remember is that the breath moving faster shouldn't *sound* breathy. If you sound uncontrollably breathy, your vocal cords are allowing too much air to escape. You should always sound like the most clear and confident version of yourself.

Mouth on My Belly

One seemingly silly visualization that works wonders for relieving vocal tension is imagining that your voice is physically coming from your stomach and vocalizing with this in mind. This quite laughable exercise works because it places all our focus right where our vocal action takes place. As stated before, vocalizing doesn't require effort from the throat and neck. Efficient vocalizing is near the diaphragm and pelvic floor. Yes, the deeper in your body you feel your energy, the better. I cannot recall any exercise that I've been taught where the teacher told me to visualize my throat or neck. They may have told me to place my hands here to ensure the external muscles stay relaxed, but as far as clean, efficient singing is concerned, focusing energy on this area of the body has little to no positive effect on how I produce my vocal tone. On the other hand, when I focus my energy deep in my belly and sing from this place, my voice feels weightless and, for lack of better words, it just feels good. Singing from this place sometimes has a sort of spiritual effect on me as well. I feel like I'm connecting to the deepest parts of my soul.

V. VOICES & REGISTERS

After about five years of teaching voice, one thing I've noticed is that students need a representation for high and low. Without it, students are just singing without any concrete, definitive knowledge as to what they're actually doing. For me, the easiest way to teach students about the highs and lows of the voice is by initially explaining, demonstrating, and showing various examples of chest and head voice.

One thing that has also aided me in my singing journey is thinking of my voice as one house that consists of a few different rooms. Our voice is one unified instrument that's made up of many different voice functions and manipulations. As you learn to sing, you'll truly amaze yourself with the various high, low, fun, creepy, and seemingly insane things you can do with your voice. The voice is one of the most complex instruments in the world!

Chest Voice

Chest voice is typically the voice we speak in. It is called chest voice because it primarily resonates in the chest cavity. If you put your hand on your collarbone and proudly say "I'm speaking in chest voice," you should feel some vibrations connecting to your hand. Thinking of cartoon giants saying "Fee-Fi-Fo-Fum" really solidified my concept of chest voice. I found that when done proudly, imitating an angry giant tends to remove excess air and noise from the chest voice. As long as this voice isn't taken too high in pitch, you can get to a pretty loud dynamic in this range without fatiguing your vocal cords.

Head Voice

Above the chest voice is our head voice. In popular music, this voice is often referred to as falsetto, and, in my personal voice lessons, I use the two terms interchangeably, especially with men. It is very common to feel like this voice is the weaker of the two. Since this isn't the voice we mainly communicate in, the muscle groups that engage in it often haven't learned how to freely coordinate yet. If you're a foundational beginner and you have no idea how to find your head voice, try hooting like an owl, saying "Wooooo!" like you're on a rollercoaster or at a concert, or talking like Mickey Mouse. For all my fellow gamers, Mario from Super Mario Bros. goes into a high head voice when he jumps and says "Yahoo!!!" Play around with these sounds and see if you recognize any more people, characters, or animals that use head voice. As long as it's comfortable and doesn't hurt, explore as much as you possibly can and feel free to email me with any findings!

The Break

When you first begin your singing journey, you'll likely have what seems like a flip or a "break" in between the two voices. Depending on your style, you may or may not like this, but for right now, embrace this flip in your voice. We will eventually learn how to make this smoother and less apparent for versatility, but for now, view this break similarly to a state sign. When you're driving and enter a new state, there's usually a sign saying, "Welcome! You're now in *insert state name here*." When you're ascending to higher notes, your break is there to let you know you have crossed over into the head voice. Likewise, when you vocalize in head voice and descend downward, your break will let you know that you have crossed over back into your chest voice. I suggest you take lots of time to get familiar with these two voices and how they sound. As long as they're comfortable, make whatever sounds you'd like. The goal is to be able to call on these sounds on command.

When I initially began taking collegiate voice lessons, I was mostly assigned classical repertoire. In this genre, men typically don't venture far outside of the chest voice range, so my falsetto voice didn't receive much attention. I was able to pull my chest voice up to sing higher than middle C, but I noticed that I started to get very vocally fatigued after singing. When I would get to F# above middle C, my chest voice felt like it would hit a ceiling and couldn't ascend any further or it would accidentally crack into a weak falsetto/head voice. This wasn't the way I intended or preferred to sing. If you experience this as well, we'll discuss solutions to this in our section about mix/middle voice. In my singing journey, mix/middle voice was the only solution that smoothed out my break; however, it was complex and took a lot of trial and error to coordinate.

VI. INTONATION

Intonation refers to your internal sense of pitch. I make strong intonation a requirement for beginner students because pitchiness exposes a lot of places where a singer can improve. I don't believe that pitchiness is an issue of nature, as much as it's an issue of function and overall trust in the instrument. All of this book's information on intonation is written under the assumption that the singer already practices efficient posture.

The reason I introduced vocal registers before intonation is because, in my experience, students who struggle with pitch tend to not be confident in the directions that their voices are supposed to go. Beginning students must be aware that when pitches ascend higher, they're going in the direction of head voice. Likewise, when pitches descend downward, they're going in the direction of chest voice. Once students understand how to make confident chest voice and head voice sounds, they naturally develop a better sense of how to find pitches in these voices.

If a singer still struggles with pitch after this, I look at their breathing. Pitchiness is often a result of not enough breath energy being released upon exhale. This could be due to nerves or unfamiliarity with the repertoire, causing the singer to not be comfortable in what they're singing, therefore, resulting in a resistant breath release. When you're confident in what you want to express, you release that expression without bounds. When you address this issue, you may not immediately find yourself making the most pleasant and beautifully efficient sounds you've ever heard, but most of my students have charted an immediate noticeable change. Regardless of whether you're singing high, low, loud, or soft, your breath should be moving energetically throughout your entire being. I find that this not only keeps me engaged as a singer but also has an interesting way of drawing a listener in. I'm not exactly sure why, but it just seems to connect.

I also find that practicing the Farinelli exercise and replacing the exhale with a singular hummed pitch works well and really gets beginners in the habit of feeling what singing with an engaged diaphragm feels like. This tackles a few goals at once by focusing on the breath cycle and comfortably producing efficiently released pitches in the mask. Once you can sustain one isolated pitch, continually repeat it until you can produce that pitch on command. Take a moment from the keyboard, guitar, or pitch detector app and come back and see if you can sustain that same pitch. Once you can do that, choose another pitch and do the same.

Target/Stream

One visualization that aids me when practicing songs is to think of the desired pitch as a target and your breath as an arrow that has to reach the target. The further out of your speaking range you go, the further away your target gets. Likewise, the faster your breath travels, the further your arrow will go.

For instance, take a moment and sing the nursery rhyme "Row, Row, Row Your Boat." If you're not familiar with it, you can find many links online. The song goes as such:

Row, row, row your boat
Gently down the stream
Merrily, merrily, merrily, merrily
Life is but a dream

Now, sing it again, but this time, notice that the very first "merrily" is higher in pitch than the rest of the song. In thinking of our target/stream exercise, this note of the song would be further away and would require you to move your exhaled tone faster in order to reach it.

Lastly, another common cause of pitchiness is inadequate closure of the vocal folds. This results in something called "hypofunctionality." Learning to sing with balanced cord closure tends to clean these issues up. Refer to the section on cord closure for more information.

VII. CORD CLOSURE

Cord closure is a pretty simple concept to understand and manipulate for your own stylistic purposes; likewise, inadequate cord closure is probably the most common issue I hear in students. Cord closure refers to how close or far apart your vocal folds come together when you vocalize. You can achieve many different effects by experimenting with various levels of cord closure. However, I learned to sing with a balanced amount of closure before venturing into other coordinations and that turned a potentially complicated singing journey into a simple one.

Peace Sign Visual

If you hold up the number two or the "peace" sign with your hand, this will give you a visual for what your vocal folds look like in your larynx. Feel free to do an internet search for a diagram of the vocal folds as well. When your index and middle finger are spread apart, this represents your vocal cords at rest with no sound coming from them.

Now, proudly say the word "one." As you say it, quickly bring your two fingers together until they touch and keep them together for as long as you hold out the word. When you inhale or return to silence, separate your fingers apart. This represents how healthy vocal cords function. When you speak or sing, the air from your lungs passes through the vocal cords, causing them to come closer together. In my singing, I find that I experience the most clarity and ease when I exercise full vocal fold closure (fingers touching.)

VOCAL FOLDS

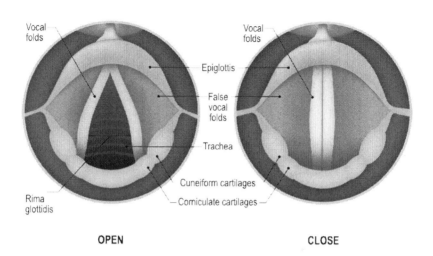

OPEN   CLOSE

Hypofunctionality

I've had the pleasure of being a consultant and teacher for singers of various ages, all at different points of their singing journey. Thus, I get passionate about this topic because I'm constantly amazed by just how many singers aren't aware that their cords aren't fully coming together. I think this is partially due to contemporary singers popularizing the breathy singing voice. When singers record in the studio, they often focus solely on capturing emotion, thus completely disregarding vocal function and efficiency. The sound of breathiness in the voice often communicates vulnerability or sensuality, which is extremely captivating in popular music, especially when sung by the female voice.

Because of this, many aspiring singers hear these records and say, "I like that sound! I want to sing like that!" They begin practicing singing with this breathy tone early in their careers, causing them to develop something called hypofunctionality. This simply means the vocal cords never fully come together and make a clear sound. With hypofunctionality, there's always an excess of breath passing through the cords. Over long periods, this can cause vocal fatigue and in rare, extreme cases, vocal damage.

I believe another culprit behind hypofunctionality is the lack of comfortable practice spaces. Before I took lessons in a studio, I only practiced in my bedroom, making sure to sing very quietly. I did this out of fear of being heard by anyone who I thought would potentially point out my mistakes. I simply hadn't built up the confidence in my voice and didn't have a safe space to build it. This caused me to develop a hypofunctional tone out of fear of being too loud. Can you relate at all? Singers who have similar experiences often believe that this soft breathiness is the full extent of their vocal tone and think they're unable to project because "that's just my voice." This is simply untrue. Hypofunctionality isn't an issue of nature. It is solely an issue of function, as the name suggests. I've had countless students who think that they possess an innate lack of projection and volume when, in reality, they just haven't learned how to completely close their cords.

My voice progressed at lightning speed when I entered an appropriate practice space. My voice teacher made me aware of my hypofunctionality and taught me efficient cord closure. Until then, I had no clue there was even another option of singing.

Balanced Cord Closure

The ideal in singing is to have a balanced amount of closure between the vocal cords. You don't want them too far apart (too much air passing through) or too compressed (not enough air passing through.) I find that the easiest way to achieve this is by starting with my speaking voice. I like to start students off making speech-like sounds because they're more familiar with them and there isn't the added pressure of having to "sing well" attached. I find that if they repeatedly say the words "you" or "one" in a comfortable speaking range, they eventually find a well-balanced amount of closure.

The key to this is to say the words clearly and confidently. I take this moment to remind students of our target and stream. In this case, we're not focused on singing pitches, but we have to aim our sound away from us, in order to speak or sing clearly. The ideal amount of distance to place your target for this exercise is about 10 feet. As you say the words "you" or "one," you should feel like your words are travelling that far.

If you sound or feel like you're closer to whispering, there's too much air in the sound. Adversely, if your throat feels tight and your voice sounds squeezed or gravelly, there isn't enough air in the sound. You shouldn't sound like any particular person or thing. You should just sound like the clearest, most confident version of yourself.

Stylistic Effect & Remembering the Core

I tell my students that any added stylistic effects they want to use can only be added after they're efficiently employing the breath cycle and singing with balanced cord closure. However, if you want to sing with a little distortion and grit, go for it! If you want to sing with some breathiness, have no fear! However, you must use these things as conscious stylistic choices. These sounds shouldn't be your default. A singer should sing with distortion and grit to communicate intensity, not because this is the only way they know to sing. Singers can use a breathy sound to come across as vulnerable, but this shouldn't be the only gear that they know to go in.

We can relate our voices to photos in the social media age. We can thank social media platforms like Instagram for introducing us to filters. Filters are simply meant to enhance the look of a photo or give it a certain effect. I believe that stylizing the voice is very much like putting a filter on it. If your original photo is low quality or taken at a bad angle, there's nothing a filter can do to change that. In relation to singing, if your breath cycle is inconsistent or your cord closure isn't balanced, you most likely will begin to feel some type of vocal fatigue once you begin to add stylistic effects such as distortion and breathiness.

I often tell my students to remember their core technical foundation. For me, my foundation consists of three elements: diaphragmatic breathing, balanced cord closure, and resonance in the mask. Diaphragmatic breathing makes sure an optimal amount of air is being supplied to the cords. Cord closure assures that the vocal cords aren't leaking air, allowing for more choices in vocal phrasing. Lastly, resonance in the mask automatically gives my voice personality and showcases my true vocal tone.

In terms of contemporary pop singers, Beyoncé Knowles is a good example of a singer who knows her core sound. When I hear her employing growls and raspiness, I always hear her clear, balanced tone underneath it all. This sound sort of works as a home base for her. This way, before she ventures into the extremes of what her voice can do, she begins with a healthy starting place.

A Note on Adequate Practice Spaces

I've found that beginning singers who are naturally comfortable practicing in a room where their family or friends are watching or listening to them are very uncommon. For this reason, vocal lessons where the student is aware that they can clearly be heard by others generally suffer and progress relatively slowly in comparison to lessons where the student perceives that they can only be heard by the teacher.

Practicing your singing voice is completely different than practicing with any other instrument. Your voice is the only instrument where you cannot visually see and correct your errors. Because of this, singers try to correct their mistakes based on what they hear, but science has proven that we don't hear ourselves as accurately as we would like to think we do. The sounds we hear when our voices resonate off the bones in our skull are much more nuanced than what's perceived by a listener in an audience. Thus, on our singing journeys, we need some sense of safety, privacy, and autonomy to explore the different ways we can feel our voice. Allow children who take singing lessons to have time to sing with no repercussions. In fact, it only helps their musical development when you encourage and have fun singing with your children. It creates an atmosphere where singing is the norm, thus making them more comfortable if they ever decide to begin professionally developing their voice.

VIII. RESONANCE

Resonance is probably one of my favorite concepts to discuss because there are a plethora of ways to resonate. In this same regard, resonance is also somewhat abstract and differs largely from person to person.

I've heard people describe resonance as where you feel your voice vibrating in your body. Personally, I think this is a bit broad, as I cannot feel my voice resonating in my left kneecap. I like to give students options, without too much room for error. With this in mind, I describe resonance as where you feel your voice vibrating in your head and face. This thought pattern gives me one general location to focus my voice, but still allows me to explore the many different ways to feel the vibrations within my skull

The Mask

There's some controversy around what it means to sing "in the mask." The way I describe the mask is rather literal. When you put on a masquerade mask, it usually covers the top half of your face. When you sing in the mask, you activate something called "nasal resonance," which means you feel internal vibrations in this area, behind the eyes and nose or behind the top row of teeth.

Here is a visual that helps me understand where to feel the vibrations of my voice.

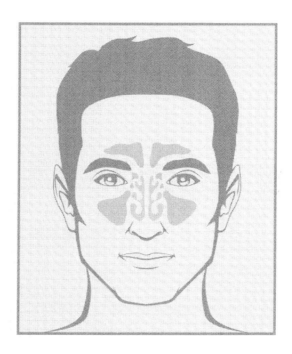

I find that singing in the mask allows for the most clarity, brightness, freedom, and effortless power in my voice. I feel each note, high or low, somewhere in the mask and when placed just right, I can sing longer phrases with ease and confidence. I'm also able to execute quicker, more precise riffs and runs, but the most rewarding benefit of this technique lies in the emotion it bears. Singing in the mask allows the underlying colors, textures, and personality of the voice to really showcase themselves.

Methods to Sing in the Mask

If you're new to this concept, here are a few things to try. Let me know what works for you or if you come up with any other ideas!

1. NG - I also refer to this as "open mouth humming." For years, I was doing scales on the NG consonant, heard in the words eNGlish, riNGiNG, or loNG. I would simply sing the word on one comfortable note very slowly until I landed on

the isolated NG sound. My throat would feel as if I were just about to make the sound of the letter K. Even now in practice, when I get to a section where I'm not sure I can comfortably get to a pitch, I'll quickly swap out the words for the NG.

2. My coach, David, encourages mask singing by simply having me pinch my nose and sing. This exercise makes me sound like Squidward Tentacles in the moment, but once I remove my hand, my voice immediately gains a bright, energetic, intentional sound. Believe it or not, this one gesture has completely reassured my sense of trust in my voice. I was recently struggling to sing some quick passages of an audition song. Once I sang the entire song with my nose pinched, my pitch accuracy immediately increased. I believe this exercise works because it places your voice in the mask to an extreme. In the moment, you virtually feel and hear your voice nowhere else. It also helps to hold a note with my nose pinched and remove my hand halfway through. The key is to fearlessly release the breath. This exercise becomes ineffective if you don't keep your breath moving fast. If there's anything I've learned from this method, it's that the most seemingly ridiculous exercises often bear the greatest results. I'll keep this in my box of warmups forever!

3. Lip Trills! This age-old vocal exercise is the go-to sound that people make when they talk about warming up and exercising the voice, and I completely see why. When done efficiently, lip trills pretty much get your entire vocal mechanism operating like a well-oiled machine. The muscles in the neck relax, the jaw releases, and your tone finds its way to the mask effortlessly. I usually begin every warm up with about 5 minutes of stretching and lip trilling. Substituting the words of a song for lip trills is also very effective as well. To lip trill, think of blowing a raspberry

except your tongue is resting inside your mouth and a constant stream of air is coming from your lips. If you can't seem to make the sound, one thing that works for my students is gently closing their mouths and repeatedly making a short "th" sound, as in the word "the." If done correctly, this won't sound like "th" because it will create the beginning of the lip trill.

Popular Singers & The Mask

Once I learned how to sing in the mask on command and what exactly it sounded like in others, I made it a point to listen to popular singers and research their relationship to mask singing. What I found is that singers who achieve extreme dynamics, flexible runs, and effortless projection all place their voices primarily in the mask. My personal favorite female examples are Aretha Franklin, Barbra Streisand, Beyoncé, Cynthia Erivo, Keke Wyatt, Whitney Houston, Sohyang, Callie Day, Lady Gaga, Julie Andrews, Yolanda Adams, and Ella Fitzgerald. This list could go on for three more pages, as I have an affinity for female voices.

Some of my male examples would be Frank Sinatra, Josh Groban, Tonex/B. Slade, Stevie Wonder, Andrea Bocelli, Ray Charles, Gregory Porter, Ben Platt, Avery Wilson, Luciano Pavarotti, Elton John, Marvin Gaye, Bryn Terfel, Smokie Norful, and Freddie Mercury. Again, this list could go on and on. More or less, I believe singers who possess versatility, control of registers, and dexterity sing in the mask.

Don't Overdo It

As with everything, it's possible to have your mask placement be too present. I find that when singers place their voice too much in the mask, their voice can become shrill and hypernasal. This is often due to their tongue bunching up in the back of their throat or their soft palate not being high enough. Thus, cutting off all airflow out of the mouth. Remember: *when singing in the mask, it's fine to imagine your voice coming out of your nose, but anatomically in singing, your breath is being released out of your mouth. Your goal is to feel a comfortable but clear balance between the two.*

IX. LARYNX

Your larynx position is another extremely important factor to be aware of because your larynx is where your vocal folds lie. I use my Adam's apple as a good indicator of where my larynx is.

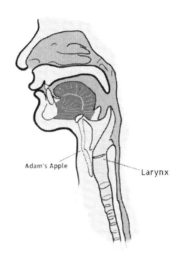

To feel your larynx move, place your hand on your Adam's apple and swallow. You should feel your larynx rise very quickly. Now, place your hand on your Adam's apple again and yawn. You should feel it quickly lower. Congratulations! You just successfully moved your larynx up and down! Play with these different larynx positions in your singing and speaking.

There are three main positions that you should explore while singing: high, low, and neutral. These three positions convey different sound qualities and aid in developing versatility in genre.

Low Larynx

Low larynx is most commonly heard in classical singing. I often hear voice teachers describe dropping the larynx as "rounding." I often hear singers without formal training refer to this as "opening up." Doing this adds a darker, fuller, and booming quality to the voice. With a low larynx, your voice will more than likely be heard. If you pull up any video of an opera singer, they'll more than likely be singing with a low larynx. In my singing journey, teachers have commonly told me to position my throat as if I were *just about* to yawn. I've found that while singing, simply emulating a yawning sensation in general can have some nice effects on vocal production as well. It should also be noted that it is possible to lower the larynx further than necessary. This can cause the voice to give off a cartoonish effect. Think Patrick Star from Spongebob Squarepants.

High Larynx

In my classical training, employing a high larynx was generally frowned upon. This is because classical singers are known for singing without amplifiers such as microphones and speakers. They use a low larynx because it communicates power and volume, which is needed to be heard over instruments and choruses. However, in contemporary music, we usually have a microphone. Therefore, singing with a low larynx 100% of the time is obsolete. I've found that the lowest part of my chest voice is most comfortable and clear with a higher larynx. The same is true for my upper mix voice as well. A high larynx position adds edginess and brightness to your vocal tone. Be conscious though. When your larynx is too high, you can block off your vocal tract and cause your vowels to "splat," which is when they spread too wide.

Neutral Larynx

Singing with a neutral larynx is amazing because it allows the singer to sound most like themselves. When we sing with a low or high larynx, it's generally because we are trying to achieve a stylized effect. With a low larynx, I'm focused on sounding powerful. With a high larynx, I'm focused on sounding edgy, but with a neutral larynx, I'm just focused on sounding like me and it requires the least amount of effort! This larynx position also tends to make me the most emotional while on stage because I'm able to deliver all my energy into communicating the lyrics.

Vomitare

One concept I overheard some opera singer friends of mine discussing is the concept of "vomitare" space. Vomitare means "to throw up" in Italian. The concept is that while singing, you shape your throat in the same position as when you throw up. I know this is a pretty bizarre concept, but trust me when I say this has worked for me and several of my students as well. The objective is to open the vocal tract and allow more sound/air to flow from the glottis. This can be further explained by thinking of the actual function of vomiting.

Functionally, vomiting takes place when the body is trying to expel something it perceives as poisonous. In the case of singing, what we should be trying to expel is air. By forming your vocal tract in this position, you lower the larynx and raise the soft palate, forming a substantial amount of space for your sound to ring out of you with little to no tension.

Classical Sounds in Contemporary Music

Once I graduated college and entered the local music scene, I noticed that many singers know how to sing with a neutral larynx and high larynx, but not a low one. I think this is mainly because people associate low laryngeal sounds with classical music. In reality, contemporary singers don't *need* to learn the low larynx position, but in terms of versatility, it only adds another layer of depth to their sound. Without low laryngeal singing, the overall sound of someone's voice won't lack clarity and beauty, but it may lack power, intensity, and depth.

My favorite contemporary singers who employ low larynxes include: Whitney Houston, Luke James, Ariana Grande, Callie Day, and Keke Wyatt.

X. MIX/MIDDLE VOICE

I intentionally saved mix (or middle) voice until later in this work because there's a lot of complexity in its definition. Mix voice allows us to access full, powerful notes in the upper range without flipping into a light, airy head voice. For this reason, many confuse this sound with belting. Learning to sing in this range will add another dimension to your voice, while also conserving your vocal energy. However, before we get into the specifics, allow me to be honest for a moment.

Personally, I believe that people get way too hung up on "finding their mix." When you do this, you focus too much on the term and not enough on the actual functionality. One thing that teachers and students often fail to recognize is that there are many different types of mixes. Mix voice is literally any amount of chest voice combined with any amount of head voice. I think that when you only describe mix as this one particular voice or sound, you neglect the other beautiful variations of it. Sometimes, you may want a heavier, chest-voice dominant mix. Other times, you may want a lighter, head-voice dominant mix. In the long run, these terms don't matter as long as you're making the sounds you want to make.

Pulled Chest Voice

Pulled chest voice is a very common mistake that singers (including myself) frequently make early in their singing journey. Since chest voice tends to be the most comfortable range we have, our brains receive positive signals from its usage. In short, when singing feels good, we want it to keep feeling good. So, when we approach a section of a song where the pitch elevates into the middle voice range, we mistakenly attempt to use the comfortable chest voice feelings to get there, thus making us uncomfortable.

The middle voice solves this issue because it acts as a bridge that crosses us over into head voice with little to no perceivability. The main thing to remember is that as we begin to venture into the middle voice, the big, heavy feelings of chest voice must taper off the higher we go. It is just physically impossible to carry all the weight of a full chest voice up into mix and head. I want to be clear in saying that chest voice doesn't fully disappear; it just lightens for the sake of ease and comfort.

How to Achieve Mixes

Note: Before attempting to sing in middle voice, I suggest becoming extremely familiar with the breath cycle and singing in the mask.

One exercise that worked for me was lip trilling in head voice and gradually descending lower and lower until I crossed over my break while remaining in head voice. If you're trying at home, make sure to repeat this four to five times before moving on. This is so your body can use head voice as a way of smoothing over the break. Once your head voice crosses over your break, you're already experiencing one form of mix voice. Once you're here, begin lip trilling in a light chest voice and ascend back toward the head voice range, but don't flip over into an airy falsetto. Stay connected to your chest voice. As you ascend, your chest voice shouldn't feel heavy and shouldn't get significantly louder, but should still be bright, ringing, and present. Over time, you should begin to feel that when you ascend, your "chest voice" is lighter, edgier, and sounds slightly nasal.

Another student of mine with a powerful mix range stated that it was easier to sing higher in mix voice when she stopped trying to intentionally be powerful and just focused on releasing her voice into that upper range. I think this is a smart way to approach this part of our voice because mix voice is already powerful on its own. It doesn't need our help. Any extra effort or push you give will only increase the risk of strain.

One method that is popular within the voice community is

vocalizing while blowing into a straw. This works well because the straw prevents you from exhausting too much air through the vocal cords. Many times, people ascend in range while doing this exercise and mistakenly think they're in a strong head voice. Because mix voice is a blend of chest voice and head voice, it is more edgy, bright, and powerful than head voice. The NG exercise mentioned in the chapter on resonance also works very similarly to this exercise and should give you a nice result as well.

The main benefit of mix voice is versatility. Once you have familiarity with the sounds and feelings of mix, you can choose which you prefer to use when the range ascends in a song. If you want to go for a lighter, more stripped back tone, head voice may be the better option. If you want to sing an attention grabbing "money note," then mixing might be the better option. That's the beauty of voice control. You get to express the way you want.

Overall, play around with these different sounds and feelings until you achieve the sound and feeling you want. If you're having difficulty getting into this range, finding a credible, well-versed vocal coach who specializes in mix voice will be beneficial.

If you're interested in hearing examples, two of my favorite mix voices come from Brendon Urie of Panic! At The Disco and Korean superstar, Sohyang. Their mix voices are powerful, yet seem to ring from them with ease.

XI. DICTION

I'll keep this section short and general because your diction changes depending on the genre/style of music and what you're trying to communicate. If you want to improve your diction for a specific genre of music, you should really invest in voice lessons with a teacher who specializes in the style, but in short, just make sure that what you're saying can clearly be heard. Stricter styles of music like musical theatre and classical require more precision with diction, while contemporary pop and certain aspects of jazz music simply don't care. At this point, contemporary singers aren't even fully completing their words, and–I can't lie–I kinda like it at times.

When I played Eddie Souther in *Sister Act*, an older gentleman stopped me after our 2nd night and said, "Your diction makes it very easy to listen to you. The way you pronounce words is a clear sign of vocal training." I always appreciate compliments like these because I remember drilling articulation during my freshman year of college. When we first began working on repertoire, Connie would stop me after every single lazily pronounced word until I realized that in singing, a sense of exaggerated speech is normal.

If You're Early, You're on Time

Have you ever heard someone say, "If you're early, you're on time; if you're on time, you're late"? If your goal is for your entire word to be heard clearly, apply the rule "If you overpronounce, you're pronouncing." I tell my students this because, in normal speech and conversation, all someone has to focus on is your tone of voice and the words you're saying. When we sing, a listener has to focus on our melodies, tone of voice, rhythms, and lyrics. If you don't fully pronounce your words in normal speech, a listener can more easily decipher what you're saying. If you don't fully pronounce while singing, you likely will just go misunderstood.

Practicing Diction

Working on diction seems tedious at first, but it takes no time to get into the swing of things. Many coaches will also take the Connie approach and immediately stop you when you don't pronounce a word clearly. Initially, this may feel frustrating, but this is to make you aware of the fact that you don't hear yourself as accurately as you think.

When I began practicing diction, I focused solely on the Italian vowels: EE, EH, AH, OH, and OO. In my current warmups, I make it a point to practice them in this order because this makes me aware of my vocal tract from the front to the back. With EH, AH, and OH, I specifically focus on opening my mouth vertically. Vowels like EH really tend to want to drag my mouth sideways. A comfortably narrow, vertical opening avoids the "splatting" sound that we discussed earlier in the book.

A few students have asked "what about EE? I can't open my mouth vertically for that." This is very true. If you tried to open your mouth vertically for an EE vowel, you would just get a mutated EH. The advice I give them is to simply press the corners of the mouth inward until they feel like they're slightly puckering and begin repeating the vowel EE from this position. You'll begin to realize that a horizontal stretch outward is not necessary to say the EE vowel. This could also be considered "covering" the vowel or "rounding it out" as well.

XII. SINGING AND THE MIND

This topic tends to give each of my students their own special flare. I typically don't teach small children, but when I do, I find that most children's imaginations allow them to sing without bounds. They often haven't yet learned to police their own thoughts and expressions. They feel their feelings and unapologetically throw them into the universe, causing them to engage with the music subjectively and deliver personally energetic performances repeatedly. Here are some nontechnical things to think about when preparing for a performance.

Imagery
This refers to the thoughts and ideas that pass through your mind while singing. Remember how I said singing is a full body experience? It requires much not only from your body but also from your creative mind and spirit. Mental images that help you connect to the story will help you sing from a deeper place and connect to the audience on a more intimate level.

One of the most common struggles I have with beginning students is they focus too much on the pitches, rhythms, and lyrics and not enough on the actual context of the underlying story. A tip Connie gave me was "In order to be a good singer, you must be a great actor." This has rung true for me frequently. Audiences may not be able to pick out all the technical mishaps, but they can absolutely decipher the difference between someone who's simply singing and someone who's storytelling.

When actors are playing a character, they often have to draw from real-life experiences, whether they be their own or inspired by the lives of others. They combine these experiences with actual research done on the character, and when executed efficiently, this makes for a truly remarkable performance.

Singers have to conjure their own mental images to create a personal relationship with the music. Another former coach of mine, Janeta Jackson, who helped me prepare for the role in Sister Act, used much of our lesson times giving me different ways to empathize with the character. My character, Eddie, was in love with the elusive and multi-talented, Deloris Van Cartier, coincidentally played by Janeta as well. Meanwhile, Eddie's sentiment isn't reciprocated by Deloris at all. Most of Eddie's scenes involved him trying to convince Deloris (and himself) that he's worthy of her love.

Janeta would often tell me to think of a time when I was attracted to someone who I didn't believe would ever feel the same for me. She would ask questions like "Was the person in another relationship?" and "How would you have felt if the person actually did like you back?" Doing this work can sometimes be difficult to revisit, but it gives you personal images that help you empathize with the character.

I Will Rejoice & Be Glad

A comment I heard from the legendary vocal pedagogue, Jo Estill, was "More people want to sing than do sing." I agree and think many singers take the activity for granted. I can't describe how many conversations I've about singing in which the person I'm speaking to says, "Oh geez, I could never do that." Every so often, I'll get an older male student who expresses that he grew up loving to sing, but chose sports instead because he thought singing was "girly." This really saddens me because singing is the main reason why I'm still alive. I found myself through finding my voice.

So many people in the world wish they could express themselves through song. They wish they had the courage to get in front of people and prove their feelings valid by singing proudly about how happy, hurt, angry, afraid, or indifferent they are. So many men would learn to be more vulnerable, if they had the chance to express vulnerability through music.

So many doors would open and so many generational curses would break. In fact, I'm breaking a few just by writing this book. Whew... I told y'all we were getting deep!

Therefore, the one feeling underneath all the techniques should be gratitude. Regardless of how you feel when you sing, rejoice in the fact that you get the chance to sing. Singing *well* just makes it that much more enjoyable. Have you ever noticed that when you get excited, your voice ascends? When you're suddenly overwhelmed with happiness, inspiration, or passion, your voice tends to elevate in pitch. Robin Hendrix, author of *How to Sing Like the Great Singers,* states, "The emotion of joy aids greatly in feeling the forward placement in the mask. It seems that this emotion moves the tiny muscles in the singing apparatus into just the right position. It empowers deeper breathing, and gives uplift to the work."

An underlying sense of joy toward singing will help you develop a closer relationship to the act of performing and an overall love for your instrument. People tend to shy away from things they don't find personal enjoyment in. This is why I make it a point to acknowledge every single time a student makes progress. When training a new skill, it's imperative that students hear "good job!" or an emphatic "yes!" This boosts their morale and reassures them that they're doing something right. This also helps build a teacher/student bond because after all, the student is trusting you with something that's woven into the imprint of their identity, their voice.

Staying Engaged

I love singing with others because with the right group of positive people, singing can become a fun, playful sport, no different from basketball, tennis, soccer, or competitive video games. In my opinion, the most important thing to remember when engaging in activities of any kind is to stay in the moment.

Listen, you don't have to tell me. I know singing can be

intense. You're trying to be aware of your body while also remembering lyrics and pitches. You keep messing up that one part no matter how many times you redo it. Then as soon as you fix THAT part, you mess up another part. It's definitely a lot, I know. However, training your mind to stay engaged in what you're doing will speed up your progress faster than you probably realize. The students who progress the slowest are the ones who monitor the way that they sound as they sing. They never fully learn to let go and trust me as a teacher because they're often afraid of sounding "bad." What they don't realize is THAT'S IT. They're not gonna die. They won't blow up the world. In a worst-case scenario, you won't make your desired sounds in front of a teacher whose job it is to take the sounds you're currently making and teach you how to make the sounds you'd like to. After each scale, they often make a twisted, confused face as if to fearfully say "was that right?" I do everything I can to break this habit early because this is the start of a mental train wreck for singers.

Once I heard a very talented basketball player say, "When I miss a free throw, I can't go 'oh man, that sucked' or else I'll take myself out of the moment. I just have to think of what I meant to do and try to do that the next time." The same exact concept applies to singing and pretty much any activity you want to be minimally decent at. When I first started singing, if my voice would miss a riff, go flat, or crack, it would really bother me in the moment. It would almost get under my skin. I would internally say, *That was trash. Why can't I sing that? I know plenty of other singers who don't even struggle with that.* Do you see how negative that is? I have now gone from enjoying the act of singing to now comparing myself to someone else's voice. The same way beautiful flowers have a hard time growing in weak, desolate soil, your singing voice has a difficult time blossoming in a negative mindset.

The way that we counteract this process is by removing the word "bad" from the conversation regarding talent. My students can attest to the fact that I don't use the word "bad" with them. I say "less efficient." When you make a mistake, remove that feeling of "Ugh!" and replace it with a feeling of "Okay. Not my best. Let me think of what I meant to do and go for that next time." This will ensure that you don't lose your cool while you're performing because I'm sure that great athletes, competitors in all fields, and salespeople will tell you that once you lose your engagement in the moment, you have an even harder time getting it back. The last thing you want to do onstage is panic or get flustered. Remember, panic causes our voices to slowly tense. You can counter this feeling by replenishing your body with a deep breath and not being so hard on yourself.

I believe that the only singing that can be categorized as bad is singing that has no intention or authenticity behind it. Talent and skill are nowhere in that conversation for me. I can't stand singers who sit in rooms and rate other singers in this way. Someone who's early in their singing journey but is relatable and has an honest story to tell is much more valuable than someone who can do tons of vocal acrobatics and has a four-octave range, but that's all they have. The more you learn about singing and voice anatomy, the more you realize that, with practice, everyone can do even the most seemingly difficult vocal acrobatics. Regular and consistent practice combined with each person's individual vocal intricacies and message virtually puts every singer on the same playing field from an appeal perspective.

XIII. RANDOM THOUGHTS

1. Stop comparing yourself to other singers. It's the easiest way to kill your morale and make you feel like your voice sucks. Listen to your vocal inspirations, but once you start beating yourself up over what you feel you can't do, CUT IT OFF!

2. Add me on Nintendo Switch! SW-2260-9909-5503

3. I learned how to sing with vibrato from listening and mimicking Beyoncé's. Thanks Bey! I'm still waiting on my orange box!

4. Drink your water! Anytime I feel my voice getting tired, rest and an overhaul of water tends to clean it up. However, don't use this as an allowance to treat your voice badly.

5. Singing = Breath Control

6. Mariah Carey's *The Emancipation of MiMi* is one of the best R&B albums to date.

7. Singing on the treadmill worked for me, but ONLY try this if you have a firm grasp on how to engage your diaphragm.

8. Whoever makes the recipe for Ben & Jerry's ice cream deserves a raise pronto! I literally can never buy just one container.

9. If you have to sing in any capacity, stay away from dairy. Your voice is Superman. Dairy is kryptonite.

10. One time, when I was about 5-years-old, my dad took me to get milkshakes, which was a very frequent occurrence for us. As you know, once you get closer to the bottom of a cup, you've drank all the sugary milk and all that's left is ice and a little water. By this point in my life, no one explained to me how gravity works. So, you can probably imagine my surprise when I eagerly turned the entire cup upside down, in hopes of enjoying the rest of the frozen delicacy and the entire milkshake fell completely over my entire face.

11. Cynthia Erivo and the cast of *The Color Purple* singing "The Color Purple (Reprise)" live on *The Today Show* changed my life for the better.

12. I'm a big believer in manifesting what you want out of life. With that said, I'll be endorsed by a major toothpaste company one day.

13. I think professionalism is a lost art and creatives need to find it sooner rather than later.

14. We need to work to remove the stigma from victims of bullying. The personal effects of bullying often carry on into adulthood, even if the person on the receiving end thinks they've gotten over it.

15. Try to take at least one day a week to sit in silence. No talking. No singing. Take this time to journal, exercise, or even do some spiritual work. When our external voices are at rest, our internal voices are communicating with the universe.

16. I believe that the best teachers are ones who can demonstrate their own techniques. Learning is a process that uses all our senses. We see our teacher's body and

posture. We hear the tone and inflections in their voice. We recreate the shape of their mouths. We breathe the way we see them breathe. We really have to start vetting our voice teachers more. Your voice is a part of your body and if you happen to lose it, it takes time to heal and, in extremely rare cases, it never does.

17. Be willing to invest in yourself. You're responsible for your own success.

18. I really hope you learned something from this book. It was a lot of fun to write and I appreciate you taking the time to read what I have to say! I'll absolutely be writing more!

Acknowledgments

I'd like to acknowledge my parents for always reassuring me that I could achieve anything I put my mind to. Many children do not grow up experiencing the amount of hope you instilled in me and it is now my goal to pass that hope along to others.

My bestfriends! You all are my second family-my chosen family. I would not have survived my darkest of times without you.

All of my Queens University of Charlotte music professors. You all laid down the foundation for everything that I currently know. I came into Queens with little musical knowledge and look at me now!

All of the loving and supportive students and families I have the honor of sharing music with. You all have been a wealth of inspiration for me and ultimately, you guys were the catalyst that started this book.

Kevin, Elizabeth, and all of my previous counselors/therapists. You have helped me realize that there is nothing wrong with expressing my thoughts. There is nothing wrong with telling my story. Thank you for allowing me to speak and be heard. It feels so free.

Dawn Anthony, Nicci Canada, and the countless other veteran performers who have invested their time and energy into me. You guys always come at the right time and say the right thing to keep me going.

All of my loyal supporters. Your love and gratitude for my content makes me want to continue this journey I'm currently on with you. We're getting through this crazy thing called life together-one step at a time.

ABOUT THE AUTHOR

Jonathan E. Smith, also known as Jay, was born and raised in Eden, NC. As a child, Jay was surrounded by the enlightening sounds of Gospel and the soulful rhythms of R&B, inspiring him to pursue a life in music. In 2017, Jay acquired his Bachelor of Arts in Music from Queens University of Charlotte, where he also learned and refined his skills in performance technique, musical theatre and classical repertoire. After completing his studies, Jay began teaching musicians of all ages the skills of voice and piano while starting an early career as a live recording artist. His sound is heavily influenced by his education and also impacted by innovative and powerhouse artists such as Whitney Houston, Luther Vandross, Beyoncé Knowles-Carter, Gregory Porter, and Toni Braxton. As a performer, Jay's mission is to inspire audiences to embrace and explore the full spectrum of their humanity, while gaining a stronger belief in themselves and what they have the potential to achieve.

Can You Help?

Thank You For Reading My Book!

I really appreciate all of your feedback, and I love hearing what you have to say!

I need your input to make the next version of this book and my future books better.

Please leave me an honest review on Amazon letting me know what you thought of the book!

Thanks so much!

Jonathan E. Smith

Printed in Poland
by Amazon Fulfillment
Poland Sp. z o.o., Wrocław